The Little Book of Dao

One liners of wisdom inspired by the Daodejing

By Reverend Deb Connor

In loving memory of Sarah Jane

Welcome to The Little Book of Dao. I invite you to contemplate these one liners of wisdom inspired by the Daodejing in whatever way you choose.

Gently ponder the message contained on each page. Some lines will immediately land with instant significance, others will percolate a while before dropping in. Your Heart and Soul will hear the message and the call from The Little Book of Dao. No matter if your head resists or tries too hard to understand and know; just let that stuff go.

Enjoy!

-Transcending-

That which may seem opposite is in fact within

Holiness and that which is wholeness both are within us

Intuition and experience come from the same place

Our experience is enriched by our intuition

Our intuition is enriched by our experience

Intuitive consciousness dissolves conscious reasoning in un-naming the named

Close the theatre
and leave the stage;
improvise the dance in
all of your life

Inflexible thinking creates stagnation of bodymind, emotions and Spirit

Embrace the spiritualization of *all* aspects of your consciousness

Transcend the unreal boundaries of art, science, religion; there find a higher consciousness

-Relativity-

Celebrate the relativity of reality

Open the door to transformation; open the door

If there is no ugly will there be no beauty?

Beauty and good need only harmony for expression; comparison becomes then unnecessary

An artist for creation of music and poetry is not required when there is beauty in the harmony of ordinary life

To teach without telling is the landscape of the wise

Care without claiming; Have without possessing; Such is to give and receive love freely

-Tempering-

By not doing, so is everything done

Desperate craving springs forth from physical, emotional and spiritual starvation

Live not in response to recompensing for deprivation; live instead in the natural expression of your life's rhythm

-The Dao-

In the endless void
lies the inexhaustible
source of all

Blunt your sharpness,
undo your tangles,
merge with the dust

What lies beyond the finite limitation of your perception?

-Yin Yang-

Existence is not sentimental; it follows not a simple wish

Yield to the rhythm, do not play by force

Put aside your ideologies for the freedom and energy of new opportunities

-Life’s Spirit-

Spirit is the infinite gateway to mystery within mystery

Always elusive while endlessly available

Cast off ideology;
Experience life
as spontaneity

Where in spiritualization of the material and materialization of the spiritual does spontaneity hide?

-Modesty-

The wise may be heard in their silence

Remain self-full through selflessness

Do not respond to the demands of your ego; find then the natural and silent serenity of fulfilment

-Highest Good-

Water nourishes life effortlessly

Water flows without prejudice

A benevolent Heart is as deep as any chasm

Goodness requires no effort or struggle when action is in natural rhythm

At the core of nature exists a highest good, at the core of human nature is it also to be found

Live in rhythm and in love rather than in the selfishness of an imbalanced ego

When good and bad are no longer opposite goodness transcends goodness

-Over fulfilment-

Keep seeking approval and you shall be chained

Over sharpen your knife and it becomes blunt

Do not overfill your bowl lest you spill it into your lap

Why purse further recognition when you have already been acknowledged?

Fulfilment is not found in more than you need

Cooperation for competition is not an exchange worth making

Now is the time to reject the excesses of our collective past

Mutually supportive and no longer in conflict; a harmonious gift to self and the other

-Limitations-

Can a true welcome to Yin be made without inviting Yang?

Seek no reward, take no pride, guide without dominating

Be ready to move, step by step

Begin this journey; begin

Transform from splinter to whole

Limitations are relative not absolute

Move out of superficial mind games and delve into the deeper vision of intuition

Do not seek to
coerce but to love
unconditionally

Do you choose the limits of rationalisation or the potential to be found in endless joy?

-Importance of what is not-

Create what is to use what is not

Use minimal effort for maximum achievement

Allow the passive to coexist with the active; just allow

Nurture and Act; Live and Love

Action need not be aggressive; Nurturing need not be passive

Even when the appearance and form of coercion changes it remains at its core coercion

Take aggression out of action and it is action not emptiness which remains

To be born of humanity and necessity is to be born in innocence

Effortless effort and contentless content has no need of excess

Dream of a world beyond wealth and poverty, defence and defencelessness, is and isn't; what lies there?

Dissolve the sides of the ditch you imagined and feel then the soft expanse of freedom

An empty mind is not the goal; a mind free of rubbish and open to harmonious content is a worthy intent

There is great difference between the end and the means

The hollow in the vessel gives space for the water, the sides of the vessel allow for the hollow; Can you drink from the hollow that has nothing to contain it?

-Choices-

The wise sacrifice the superficial for the essential

Notice the relative importance of the inner compared to the outer

Do not destroy your senses with excesses

-Identity-

Praise and criticism can both be harmful

Love the world as yourself and all reality becomes your haven

To an insecure ego each accolade generates a need for an even greater honour

In the presence of low self-esteem even the slightest criticism becomes a mountain of limitation

Knowing yourself to be part of the universe means neither success nor failure hold any power over you

Transform ego-identity to community-identity and find there a joyful path

-Beyond Reason-

What use do we have for anything when we are so obsessed with acquiring possessions?

Re-enter your life through the open doorway that is harmony with nature

-Ancient Times-

Be cautious when crossing an icy stream

Never seeking fulfilment means never being unfulfilled

The closer we come to grasping it the further away it seems

Can you remain still
while the muddy
water clears

-Tranquility-

Without tranquillity action is blind; a sure path to disaster

-Leaders-

When things happen naturally no one presumes to take the credit

-Paradoxes-

Consume only the needs of your body and Soul

When there is no longer deprivation then charity has no meaning

Question your ideology do you use it to justify inequality?

Recreate and live consciously; this is your unique capability

Embrace simplicity and integrity

Allow love and concern for others to define you

-Sorrow of Unfulfilment-

The greater the volume of trivia the louder the anxiety

Giving yourself a liberal sounding name is only a pretence of siding with the people

To appreciate doubt
first be certain

The wise do not boast and are therefore appreciated, they do not announce their superiority and are therefore acclaimed

If you do not compete then no one can compete with you

Artify the science and in that same moment scientify the art

$e=mc^2$ said my lover;
such is Dao said I

10% of profit from this book will be donated to the OneSpirit Interfaith Foundation bursary fund to help students with low or no income access interfaith ministerial training.

About the author

Reverend Deb Connor MBAcC

Rev Deb is a OneSpirit Interfaith Foundation Minister, TCM Acupuncturist, Meditation/ Qi Gong Teacher, Spiritual Counsellor, Workshop & Retreat Leader, Lovely Vegan, all round good falafel and 'big sister' to all. She lives in St Helens. Merseyside UK where her acupuncture and spiritual counselling practice is based. She runs retreats and workshops worldwide and online. Her 6 month course

'The Growth and Encouragement Programme' incorporates Deb's extensive knowledge and experience of Chinese Medicine & Daoism; The Enneagram; The 12 Steps of Recovery and A Course in Miracles. It encourages participants to move forward in all aspects of their life by deepening into their spirituality. Rev Deb is enthusiastic about life! She lives what she teaches with genuine compassion and peaceful tranquillity. She is immensely passionate about her work, which is evident in the fun, joy and heartfelt love she infuses into everything. Find out more about Rev Deb and her work at www.lovelyvegan.co.uk

33677638R00077

Printed in Great Britain
by Amazon